8 Steps to Succeeding as a Professional Tax Preparer

Felissia Petite

Table Of Contents

Introduction

Introducing "8 Steps to Succeeding as a Professional Tax Preparer" – a compelling book crafted by none other than myself Felissia Petite. In this book, I break down the necessary knowledge that encouraged me to write about the eight steps essential for achieving success in the world of tax preparation. These very steps were the foundation of my own journey, leading me to become a thriving and accomplished tax preparer.

Motivated by the desire to provide for my family during the challenging times of the Covid-19 pandemic, I sought out avenues that would offer me the financial stability we needed. It was during this pursuit that I had the good fortune of crossing paths with Nicole Mason, who is a big deal in the tax industry. Nicole became an invaluable mentor who not only guided me but also provided me with an incredible advantage—a shortcut to learning the intricacies of the tax industry.

Having personally experienced the transformative power of these eight steps, I felt compelled to share my knowledge and insights with others who aspire to embark on a similar path. This book serves as a roadmap, carefully outlining the vital steps required to excel as a professional tax preparer.

STEP 1: Learning the Tax Industry (Finding training and courses)

Once I got next to Nicole Mason and took my proper training and courses to learn the ins and outs about the tax industry it really helped alot with the process. You have to find yourself a good trainer who really makes sure you understand and wants to see you win. I always do my research on who I chose to work with and she ended up a great pick for me since she's not only in it for herself but to actually build a team and build others around her. She is now my Mentor and continues to help me through my whole tax business to become successful. So it is very important that you do your research as I did on a good trainer who will work with you in the long run and not to only help themselves. A great trainer is not just a teacher, but a guide, motivator, and catalyst for transformation.

When it comes to finding training and courses for tax preparers, there are several options available to you. Here are some steps you can take to get started:

1. Research reputable organizations: Look for established organizations that offer tax preparer training programs. Some well-known organizations in the United States include the National Association of Tax Professionals (NATP), the National Society of Accountants (NSA), and the Internal Revenue Service (IRS).

2. Check local educational institutions: Many community colleges and vocational schools offer tax preparation courses. Explore their course catalogs or reach out to their business or accounting departments to inquire about tax preparation programs they offer.

3. Online courses and webinars: There are numerous online platforms and websites that provide tax preparer training. Examples include Udemy, Coursera, and TaxMama. Also people like myself who are in your local community who are certified and know a lot about the tax industry with years experience. Make sure to review the course content, instructor qualifications, and user reviews before making a decision.

4. IRS resources: The IRS offers various training resources for tax professionals, including webinars, online courses, and workshops. Visit their website (www.irs.gov) and navigate to the "Tax Professionals" section to explore the available options.

5. Networking and professional organizations: Connect with professionals in the tax industry through networking events, seminars, or joining professional organizations. These connections can lead to valuable insights and recommendations for training programs.

6. Certification programs: Consider pursuing professional certifications such as the Enrolled Agent (EA) designation, Certified Public Accountant (CPA), or Certified Financial Planner (CFP). These certifications often require comprehensive training and passing exams, which can enhance your credibility as a tax preparer.

Remember to assess the course content, cost, flexibility, and accreditation of the programs you consider. It's also beneficial to choose courses that cover the specific tax regulations and laws relevant to your region or country.

STEP 2: Write Out a Business Plan (How do I want my business to run, who am I targeting to become a part of my team)

A person with a well-crafted business plan is like an architect who lays a strong foundation for success, building dreams into reality with every calculated step. The way I wrote my business plan was by sitting down writing out how I wanted to run my business and who I was targeting. I wrote down the type of people I wanted to be affiliated with and which rooms I wanted to be in so that my business could prosper. I made sure my business would be ran very professionally giving my clients the best customer service they could receive.

- Importance of a Business Plan in the Tax Industry and understanding your target audience

1. Roadmap for Success: A well-crafted business plan serves as a roadmap for your tax business. It outlines your goals, strategies, and actions required to achieve them. It provides a clear direction and helps you stay

focused on your objectives, ultimately increasing your chances of success.

2. Understanding the Market: A business plan requires market research, allowing you to gain a deep understanding of the tax industry, including trends, competition, and client needs. This knowledge enables you to identify opportunities, target specific market segments, and position your services effectively.

3. Financial Planning and Management: Developing a business plan involves financial forecasting, budgeting, and projections. It helps you estimate your startup costs, operational expenses, revenue streams, and potential profitability. This financial planning allows you to make informed decisions, secure financing if needed, and effectively manage your finances.

4. Identifying Target Clients and Services: A business plan helps you define your target clients, their demographics, and their specific tax needs. It allows you to tailor your services to meet those needs and develop a compelling value proposition that differentiates you from competitors. Understanding your target clients is crucial for effective marketing and client acquisition.

5. Competitive Analysis: Through a business plan, you conduct a comprehensive analysis of your competition in the tax industry. This analysis helps you identify their strengths, weaknesses, and unique selling points. Understanding your competitors allows you to develop strategies to differentiate yourself, capitalize on market gaps, and provide a superior service.

6. Operational Efficiency: A business plan includes details about your operational structure, workflow processes, and resource requirements. It helps you streamline your operations, identify potential bottlenecks, and implement efficient systems and technologies to optimize productivity. By improving operational efficiency, you can enhance client satisfaction and maximize profitability.

7. Risk Assessment and Mitigation: Developing a business plan requires you to assess potential risks and challenges your tax business may face. This allows you to proactively identify and mitigate risks, ensuring continuity and minimizing disruptions. It also helps you devise contingency plans and strategies to handle unforeseen circumstances.

8. Communication and Collaboration: A business plan serves as a communication tool when seeking funding,

partnerships, or collaborations. It provides a comprehensive overview of your tax business, its goals, and its potential. Sharing your business plan with stakeholders demonstrates professionalism, strategic thinking, and your commitment to success.

A business plan is vital in the tax industry as it provides a roadmap for success, helps you understand the market.

- Understanding Your Target Audience

Understanding your target audience in the tax industry is of utmost importance due to the following reasons:

1. Tailored Services: When you have a deep understanding of your target audience, you can tailor your services specifically to their needs. Different client segments may have distinct tax requirements, preferences, and pain points. By understanding your target audience, you can customize your services, provide relevant solutions, and address their specific challenges effectively.

2. Effective Marketing: Knowing your target audience allows you to develop and implement targeted marketing strategies. You can create compelling messaging, choose appropriate marketing channels, and craft campaigns that resonate with your audience. This

focused approach increases the likelihood of attracting the right clients, maximizing your marketing efforts, and generating higher quality leads.

3. Client Acquisition and Retention: Understanding your target audience helps you identify potential clients who are most likely to benefit from your services. This enables you to concentrate your efforts on acquiring these clients, saving time and resources. Additionally, by tailoring your services to meet their needs, you increase the chances of client satisfaction and loyalty, promoting long-term relationships and repeat business.

4. Differentiation from Competitors: In a competitive tax industry, understanding your target audience gives you a competitive edge. By identifying the unique needs and pain points of your audience, you can differentiate your services from competitors. This allows you to offer specialized expertise, unique value propositions, and personalized solutions that align with your target audience's requirements.

5. Efficient Resource Allocation: Understanding your target audience helps optimize resource allocation. By focusing on specific client segments, you can allocate your time, energy, and marketing budget more effectively. This prevents wasted efforts on unqualified

leads and allows you to direct resources where they will have the greatest impact.

6. Enhanced Client Communication: Knowing your target audience enables you to communicate effectively with your clients. You can use language and messaging that resonates with them, address their concerns, and provide clear and relevant information. This promotes better client engagement, satisfaction, and overall client experience.

7. Anticipating Industry Trends: Understanding your target audience helps you stay informed about the evolving needs and preferences in the tax industry. By monitoring market trends and staying connected with your audience, you can anticipate changes in tax regulations, emerging technologies, and client expectations. This positions you as a proactive advisor, allowing you to offer relevant and timely services.

8. Continuous Improvement: Regularly understanding and assessing your target audience enables you to gather feedback, identify areas for improvement, and refine your services. By actively seeking client input and adapting to their evolving needs, you can enhance your service offerings, stay competitive, and foster long-term client satisfaction.

Understanding your target audience in the tax industry is essential for tailoring services, effective marketing, client acquisition and retention, differentiation from competitors, efficient resource allocation, enhanced client communication, anticipating industry trends, and continuous improvement. By deeply understanding your target audience, you can position your tax business for success and deliver services that meet their unique needs.

STEP 3: Licensing Needed (PTIN / EFIN etc…)

Obtaining licensing is not just a formality, but a testament to the commitment, expertise, and unwavering pursuit of excellence that sets individuals apart as true professionals in their field. My trainer instructed me on the importance of having licensing in the tax industry and I know PTIN AND EFIN are two licensing I would need to be able to file taxes legally. After I registered for those licenses I felt good about it because as I said before I want to be as professional as possible and one thing that comes with being professional is doing things the legal way being licensed.

#1: Preparer Tax Identification Number (PTIN)

1.1 What is a PTIN?

1.2 Why do tax professionals need a PTIN?

1.3 How to obtain a PTIN?

1.4 Renewing and updating your PTIN

1.5 PTIN requirements and responsibilities

A PTIN, or Preparer Tax Identification Number, is a unique identification number issued by the Internal Revenue Service (IRS) to tax return preparers. The PTIN is required for individuals who prepare or assist in preparing federal tax returns for compensation. It is a way for the IRS to track and regulate tax professionals who provide tax preparation services.

Obtaining a PTIN is necessary for tax preparers to meet their tax filing obligations and comply with IRS regulations. It helps ensure accountability, professionalism, and accuracy in tax preparation services. Tax professionals are required to include their PTIN on all tax returns they prepare or assist in preparing.

To obtain a PTIN, tax preparers need to complete an application process with the IRS, which includes providing personal information, paying a fee, and meeting certain eligibility requirements. The IRS issues the PTIN as a unique identifier that is used to track and identify tax preparers in their interactions with the IRS.

It's important for tax professionals to maintain an active PTIN and keep it up to date. The PTIN must be renewed annually, and any changes to personal information or circumstances should be promptly reported to the IRS.

Failure to comply with PTIN requirements may result in penalties or other consequences.

Overall, a PTIN is a unique identification number assigned to tax preparers by the IRS, and it is an important requirement for individuals who provide tax preparation services and assist taxpayers in filing their federal tax returns.

#2: Electronic Filing Identification Number (EFIN)

2.1 What is an EFIN?

2.2 Importance of an EFIN for tax professionals

2.3 Obtaining an EFIN

2.4 Maintaining and renewing your EFIN

2.5 EFIN safeguards and security measures

EFIN stands for Electronic Filing Identification Number. It is a unique identification number assigned by the Internal Revenue Service (IRS) to authorized electronic return originators (EROs) and transmitters. An EFIN allows tax professionals to electronically file tax returns with the IRS on behalf of their clients.

The EFIN is necessary for tax professionals who wish to participate in the IRS e-file program, which enables the electronic submission of tax returns, including individual, business, and other types of tax filings. EROs and transmitters use their EFIN to electronically sign and transmit tax returns securely to the IRS.

To obtain an EFIN, tax professionals must go through an application process with the IRS, which involves providing personal information, business details, and demonstrating compliance with IRS requirements for e-file providers. The IRS reviews the application and, if approved, assigns a unique EFIN to the tax professional.

Having an EFIN allows tax professionals to offer the convenience and efficiency of electronic filing to their clients. It streamlines the tax preparation process, reduces paperwork, and speeds up the processing and refund issuance timeframes for eligible taxpayers.

It's important for tax professionals to safeguard their EFIN and use it responsibly. The EFIN should only be used for authorized electronic filing purposes and in compliance with IRS guidelines. Tax professionals must also comply with IRS requirements for record retention, security, and privacy when handling electronic tax return information.

In summary, an EFIN is a unique identification number issued by the IRS to authorized electronic return originators and transmitters. It enables tax professionals to electronically file tax returns on behalf of their clients, providing faster processing and improved efficiency in the tax preparation process.

#3: Responsibilities and Best Practices with having these licenses

1: Ethical responsibilities of tax professionals

Tax professionals have ethical responsibilities that guide their conduct and interactions with clients, the tax authorities, and the public. These responsibilities are important for maintaining professional integrity and ensuring compliance with laws and regulations. Here are some key ethical responsibilities of tax professionals:

1. Competence: Tax professionals are responsible for maintaining a high level of competence in their field. This includes staying updated with changes in tax laws, regulations, and accounting practices. They should strive to provide accurate and reliable tax advice and services to clients based on their expertise and knowledge.

2. Confidentiality: Tax professionals have a duty to maintain the confidentiality of client information. They should not disclose any client-related information to third parties without the client's consent, except when required by law or professional standards. Safeguarding client confidentiality helps build trust and ensures the privacy of sensitive financial and personal information.

3. Independence and Objectivity: Tax professionals should maintain independence and objectivity in their professional judgments. They should avoid conflicts of interest that could compromise their ability to provide unbiased advice or services. Independence ensures that tax professionals act in the best interest of their clients and uphold the integrity of the tax system.

4. Professionalism and Integrity: Tax professionals should adhere to high standards of professionalism and integrity in their interactions with clients, colleagues, and the public. They should be honest, truthful, and transparent in their communication and conduct. Professionalism encompasses ethical behavior, respectful treatment of clients, and compliance with professional codes of conduct.

5. Compliance with Laws and Regulations: Tax professionals have a responsibility to comply with all applicable laws, regulations, and professional standards governing their practice. They should ensure that their tax advice and services align with legal requirements and promote lawful behavior. This includes providing accurate tax returns, reporting income and deductions correctly, and avoiding any illegal tax schemes or evasion.

6. Continuing Education and Professional Development: Tax professionals should engage in continuous learning and professional development to enhance their knowledge and skills. They should actively pursue opportunities for education and training to stay updated with changes in tax laws, regulations, and industry practices. Ongoing professional development ensures that tax professionals deliver high-quality services and maintain their competence.

By adhering to these ethical responsibilities, tax professionals can uphold the trust and confidence of their clients, contribute to a fair and transparent tax system, and maintain the integrity of the tax profession.

2: Staying up-to-date with tax laws and regulations

Staying up to date with tax laws and regulations is crucial for tax professionals to effectively serve their clients and maintain compliance. Here are some reasons why staying current with tax laws is important:

1. Accuracy in Tax Compliance: Tax laws and regulations are subject to frequent changes at the local, state, and federal levels. Staying up to date helps tax professionals accurately interpret and apply tax laws when preparing

tax returns, ensuring that clients' tax obligations are met and avoiding potential errors or penalties.

2. Compliance with Filing Deadlines: Tax laws dictate specific deadlines for filing tax returns and making tax payments. Being aware of these deadlines and any changes helps tax professionals ensure that their clients' tax obligations are fulfilled on time. Timely compliance avoids late filing penalties and unnecessary complications.

3. Maximizing Tax Savings: Tax laws often include provisions that allow taxpayers to claim deductions, credits, or other tax benefits. By staying informed about these provisions, tax professionals can identify opportunities for clients to maximize their tax savings and take advantage of available tax incentives.

4. Effective Tax Planning: Staying current with tax laws and regulations enables tax professionals to provide proactive tax planning strategies for their clients. They can identify potential tax implications related to changes in tax codes, advise clients on the tax consequences of specific financial decisions, and help them plan their finances in a tax-efficient manner.

5. Compliance with Ethical and Professional Standards: Tax professionals have ethical and professional responsibilities to provide accurate and reliable tax advice. Staying updated with tax laws and regulations is essential for meeting these responsibilities and ensuring that clients receive accurate and up-to-date guidance.

6. Adapting to Legislative Changes: Tax laws can be influenced by changes in government policies, economic conditions, or societal needs. Staying informed allows tax professionals to understand the rationale behind legislative changes and adapt their strategies accordingly. They can help clients navigate new requirements, comply with revised regulations, and adjust their tax planning approaches.

To stay up to date with tax laws and regulations, tax professionals engage in various activities such as attending professional training programs, participating in continuing education courses, joining industry associations, subscribing to tax publications, and actively monitoring updates from tax authorities. By prioritizing ongoing learning and staying current, tax professionals can provide valuable services to their clients while ensuring compliance with the ever-evolving tax landscape.

3: Protecting client information and privacy

Protecting client information and privacy is of utmost importance in the tax business. Tax professionals handle sensitive financial and personal information, and safeguarding this data is essential for maintaining client trust and complying with legal and ethical obligations. Here are some key considerations for protecting client information and privacy:

1. Secure Data Storage: Use secure methods to store and protect client information. Implement physical safeguards, such as locked cabinets or secure storage rooms, to prevent unauthorized access to physical documents. For electronic data, employ robust security measures like encryption, firewalls, and secure servers to safeguard against cyber threats.

2. Access Control: Limit access to client information on a need-to-know basis. Implement user authentication and access control measures to ensure that only authorized individuals can access sensitive data. Regularly review and update access permissions based on staff roles and responsibilities.

3. Employee Training and Awareness: Provide comprehensive training to employees on data privacy

and security protocols. Educate them about the importance of client confidentiality, the risks of data breaches, and the appropriate handling and disposal of client information. Foster a culture of privacy awareness and instill a sense of responsibility among employees.

4. Secure Communication Channels: Use secure communication methods when transmitting client information. Encourage the use of encrypted email services or client portals for sharing sensitive documents and information. Discourage the use of insecure channels, such as regular email or unencrypted messaging platforms, for discussing client matters.

5. Data Backup and Recovery: Regularly back up client data to ensure its availability and integrity. Implement robust backup systems and test the recovery process periodically to mitigate the risk of data loss or corruption. Consider storing backups in secure off-site locations to protect against physical damage or disasters.

6. Compliance with Privacy Laws and Regulations: Familiarize yourself with applicable privacy laws, such as the General Data Protection Regulation (GDPR) or the Health Insurance Portability and Accountability Act (HIPAA), depending on the nature of the client information you handle. Understand your obligations

regarding data collection, storage, sharing, and disclosure, and ensure compliance with relevant regulations.

7. Secure Disposal of Information: Develop and implement protocols for the secure disposal of client information. Shred physical documents containing sensitive data before discarding them. Ensure that electronic data is permanently and securely erased from devices or storage media before disposal or reuse.

8. Confidentiality Agreements: Establish confidentiality agreements with clients to reinforce their trust and commitment to protecting their information. These agreements outline the responsibilities of both parties in maintaining confidentiality and set expectations for how client information will be handled.

By implementing robust privacy and data protection practices, tax professionals can demonstrate their commitment to safeguarding client information and privacy. Protecting client data not only strengthens client relationships but also helps prevent the risk of data breaches, identity theft, and regulatory non-compliance, thereby preserving the integrity and reputation of the tax business.

4: Maintaining professionalism and accuracy in tax filings

Maintaining professionalism and accuracy in tax filings is essential for tax professionals in the tax business. It not only ensures compliance with legal and ethical obligations but also builds trust with clients and upholds the integrity of the tax system. Here are some key considerations for maintaining professionalism and accuracy in tax filings:

1. Knowledge and Competence: Stay updated with the latest tax laws, regulations, and accounting practices. Continuously enhance your knowledge through professional development programs, seminars, and ongoing education. This ensures that you have the necessary expertise to accurately interpret and apply tax laws when preparing tax filings.

2. Attention to Detail: Pay meticulous attention to detail when gathering client information, preparing tax returns, and reviewing supporting documentation. Avoid overlooking important details or making careless errors that could impact the accuracy of the tax filings. Double-check calculations, verify data, and conduct thorough reviews to minimize mistakes.

3. Compliance with Filing Requirements: Familiarize yourself with the filing requirements specific to each type of tax return and ensure compliance with applicable deadlines. Stay informed about any changes in filing requirements and submission procedures to avoid delays or penalties. Accurately complete all necessary forms, schedules, and disclosures as required by the tax authorities.

4. Documentation and Record-Keeping: Maintain organized and accurate records of client information, supporting documents, and tax filings. Keep copies of all relevant documents, such as W-2s, 1099s, receipts, and invoices, to support the information reported on tax returns. Proper documentation not only facilitates accurate filings but also helps in case of audits or inquiries.

5. Professional Ethics and Standards: Adhere to high standards of professionalism, integrity, and ethical conduct in your tax practice. Comply with the professional codes of conduct established by regulatory bodies or industry associations. Act in the best interest of your clients, avoid conflicts of interest, and maintain client confidentiality and privacy.

6. Quality Control and Review Processes: Implement internal quality control measures to ensure accuracy and consistency in tax filings. Establish review processes that involve independent review by another qualified professional to catch any errors or inconsistencies before finalizing the tax filings. This adds an extra layer of assurance and reduces the risk of inaccuracies.

7. Communication and Client Engagement: Maintain clear and open lines of communication with clients. Explain tax concepts, obligations, and the information required from clients in a clear and understandable manner. Foster a collaborative relationship with clients to address any questions or concerns they may have and provide accurate guidance tailored to their specific circumstances.

8. Professional Liability Insurance: Consider obtaining professional liability insurance to protect against potential errors, omissions, or negligence claims arising from your tax services. This insurance coverage provides financial protection and can offer peace of mind when providing tax-related advice and services.

By maintaining professionalism and accuracy in tax filings, tax professionals demonstrate their commitment to providing high-quality services and ensuring compliance with tax laws. This not only benefits clients but also helps to maintain the reputation and credibility of the tax business in the industry.

Obtaining and maintaining the necessary licenses, such as the PTIN and EFIN, is crucial for tax professionals to provide quality tax services and ensure compliance with legal and ethical standards. By understanding the requirements and responsibilities associated with these licenses, you can confidently navigate the tax industry and serve your clients effectively.

STEP 4: Tax Software (Which Software is right for me & provides the best benefit)

I looked around quite a bit for Softwares best for my company that provided my team with great benefits. The tax software I chose to work with turned out great for me because it provided benefits like 24 hour tech support, great pricing, easy filing and more. Some softwares don't come with a lot of good benefits so make sure to do your research like I did to see which one is best for you.

Efficiency and Time Savings: The right tax software can streamline the tax preparation process, automating calculations and reducing manual data entry. This efficiency translates into significant time savings, allowing tax professionals to serve more clients and handle complex tax scenarios efficiently.

Accuracy and Compliance: Tax software often comes equipped with built-in tax law databases and automatic updates, ensuring compliance with the latest tax regulations. This helps minimize errors and reduces the risk of non-compliance, avoiding penalties and potential legal issues.

Enhanced Productivity: Advanced tax software offers features like data import/export, document management, and e-filing capabilities, enabling tax professionals to handle higher volumes of tax returns effectively. Such tools eliminate repetitive tasks, improve workflow, and enhance overall productivity.

Client Collaboration and Communication: Many tax software solutions include features that facilitate collaboration and communication with clients. These can include secure client portals, document sharing, and real-time messaging, enabling seamless interaction, data exchange, and transparency throughout the tax preparation process.

Cost Savings: Although tax software typically involves an upfront investment or subscription cost, the long-term benefits often outweigh the expense. By automating manual processes, reducing errors, and increasing efficiency, tax software helps save costs associated with labor, rework, and potential penalties due to errors.

Data Security and Privacy: Reputable tax software providers prioritize data security, offering robust encryption, secure data storage, and access controls. This ensures the confidentiality and integrity of sensitive client information, safeguarding against potential data breaches and identity theft.

Scalability and Adaptability: The right tax software should be scalable to accommodate your growing client base and adapt to changing tax regulations. It should offer updates and enhancements to keep pace with industry standards, ensuring your software remains reliable and up-to-date.

Reporting and Analytics: Advanced tax software often provides reporting and analytics capabilities, offering valuable insights into your tax practice's performance, client trends, and profitability. These features can aid in decision-making, identifying areas for improvement, and optimizing your business operations.

In summary, finding the right tax software is essential to leverage technology effectively and gain numerous advantages in the tax industry, including increased efficiency, accuracy, productivity, client collaboration, cost savings, data security, scalability, adaptability, and valuable reporting capabilities.

STEP 5: Marketing Strategies (How will I get my services out to reach more clients)

Marketing strategies are the brushstrokes of influence, weaving captivating narratives and painting vivid paths that lead businesses towards success and hearts towards conviction. The marketing strategies I used were mainly through social media. I ran business ads to reach more people, I posted my flyer and happy customer results everyday during tax seasons and I baited people in with a good offering to them if they filed with me. I told people if they filed with me I would give them Free credit repair from my Husband who runs his own credit repair company which worked out in my favor. If you have any other side businesses offer your clients something free from your other business or partner up with someone that has a service you would like to give your customers for free and work out a deal with that partnership. I also hired a Virtual Assitant to help posting some content because sometimes it gets overwhelming trying to do it all by yourself !

1. Attracting New Clients: Marketing strategies help you reach a wider audience and attract potential clients to

your tax preparation services. By utilizing various marketing channels such as online advertising, social media, search engine optimization (SEO), and targeted campaigns, you can increase brand visibility and generate leads.

2. Building Brand Awareness: Marketing allows you to establish and build brand awareness in your target market. By consistently promoting your tax preparation business, highlighting your unique value proposition, and showcasing your expertise, you can differentiate yourself from competitors and create recognition and trust among potential clients.

3. Expanding Client Base and Retention: Marketing efforts not only help attract new clients but also contribute to client retention and referral generation. By staying engaged with existing clients through newsletters, email marketing, and personalized communications, you can nurture relationships, encourage repeat business, and stimulate referrals.

4. Showcasing Expertise and Credibility: Effective marketing strategies enable you to showcase your tax expertise and establish credibility in the industry. By providing valuable content through blog posts, webinars, or educational resources, you position yourself as a

knowledgeable authority, earning the trust of potential clients.

5. Adapting to Industry Changes: Marketing strategies help you stay relevant and adapt to evolving trends in the tax industry. By keeping up with market research, competitor analysis, and customer feedback, you can identify opportunities, anticipate changing client needs, and adjust your marketing messages and offerings accordingly.

6. Differentiating from Competitors: The tax industry can be highly competitive, and effective marketing allows you to differentiate yourself from other tax preparers. By identifying your unique selling points, crafting compelling messaging, and emphasizing your strengths, you can stand out in the market and attract clients who align with your value proposition.

7. Enhancing Online Presence: In today's digital age, having a strong online presence is essential. Marketing strategies such as website optimization, online reviews, and social media management contribute to a positive online reputation and help potential clients find and engage with your tax preparation business easily.

8. Maximizing Return on Investment (ROI): Implementing targeted marketing strategies allows you to optimize your marketing budget and achieve a higher return on investment. By measuring and analyzing the effectiveness of different marketing campaigns, you can allocate resources to the most successful channels and tactics.

In summary, marketing strategies are vital for a tax preparation business to attract new clients, build brand awareness, retain existing clients, establish credibility, adapt to industry changes, differentiate from competitors, enhance online presence, and maximize ROI. By effectively promoting your services, you can expand your client base, foster long-term relationships, and ultimately drive business growth.

STEP 6: Best Tools For Smooth Filing (Implement efficiency tools that can be used for smoother process like E-sign for tax return signings, secure client sign up "Taxes To Go App", paperless document storage)

The main tools I had for my clients to use to make filing easier, smoother and worry free was the "Taxes to go app". This app came in handy for a lot of my clients who wanted to feel safer with their documents to upload and it also made it easier for me when the documentation uploads already into my system and I don't have to do it manually.

1. Enhanced Efficiency: These tools streamline the tax preparation process and save valuable time. The Taxes To Go app allows clients to securely upload their tax documents and provide necessary information remotely, reducing the need for in-person meetings or physical document exchange. E-signature software eliminates the need for printing, signing, and scanning paper

documents, making the signing process quick and convenient. Paperless document storage eliminates the need for physical filing cabinets, enabling easy organization, retrieval, and sharing of client files.

2. Improved Client Experience: Utilizing these tools improves the client experience by offering convenience, flexibility, and accessibility. Clients can conveniently submit their tax information through the Taxes To Go app at their convenience, eliminating the need for in-person visits or paper-based processes. E-signatures allow clients to sign tax returns remotely, avoiding the need for physical meetings and increasing convenience. Paperless document storage ensures that clients' files are easily accessible whenever needed, providing a smooth and efficient service experience.

3. Data Security and Compliance: These tools often come equipped with robust security measures to protect sensitive client information. The Taxes To Go app ensures secure data transmission and storage, reducing the risk of data breaches. E-signature software employs encryption and authentication protocols to safeguard client signatures and tax documents. Paperless document storage systems typically offer encryption, access controls, and regular backups, ensuring

compliance with data protection regulations and minimizing the risk of data loss.

4. Cost Savings: By utilizing these tools, tax professionals can reduce expenses associated with physical storage, printing, and document handling. Paperless document storage eliminates the need for physical storage space and associated costs. E-signature software reduces printing and mailing costs for tax return signings. These cost savings can contribute to the overall profitability of your tax preparation business.

5. Environmentally Friendly: Adopting paperless processes contributes to environmental sustainability by reducing paper usage and waste. By utilizing the Taxes To Go app and paperless document storage, you can significantly reduce your carbon footprint and promote eco-friendly practices.

6. Scalability and Collaboration: These tools support scalability as your tax business grows. The Taxes To Go app can handle increasing numbers of client submissions without physical constraints. E-signature software allows for seamless collaboration with remote clients, ensuring efficient signing processes regardless of geographical location. Paperless document storage facilitates easy collaboration among team members,

enabling simultaneous access to client files and improving workflow efficiency.

In summary, leveraging the best tools in the tax industry, such as the Taxes To Go app, e-signature software for tax return signings, and paperless document storage, offers benefits including enhanced efficiency, improved client experience, data security and compliance, cost savings, environmental sustainability, scalability, and collaboration. By incorporating these tools into your tax preparation process, you can optimize operations, deliver a high-quality service, and stay ahead in a competitive industry.

STEP 7: Satisfy Clients (Answer Questions, staying in contact with clients, Ensuring them of each taxes update, making sure they feel comfortable throughout the entire process)

The things I did to ensure my clients were satisfied included me letting them know each tax update, making sure I stay in contact and reachable, keeping my professional image . You want to make sure you give the best customer service so that your clients want to keep returning to you. You better believe if they didn't like your customer service they will not return. also what I did to satisfy my clients was giving them a free trip voucher something other companies aren't providing so that makes them feel like they came to the right company to file their taxes. I checked for clients updates everyday and sent out new information that I see and also stayed true and transparent.

*Retaining Clients and Building Loyalty: By staying in regular contact with clients and keeping them informed about tax updates, you demonstrate your commitment to their financial well-being. This builds trust and loyalty, increasing the likelihood of repeat business and referrals.

*Meeting Client Expectations: Proactively staying in touch with clients and keeping up with their tax updates ensures that you meet their expectations. Clients appreciate timely and relevant communication, as it helps them stay informed about changes that may impact their financial situations.

*Enhancing Client Experience: Effective communication and staying connected with clients throughout the tax preparation process enhance the overall client experience. Regular updates, personalized interactions, and addressing their concerns contribute to a positive and comfortable experience, fostering long-term relationships.

*Providing Peace of Mind: Tax matters can be complex and stressful for clients. By keeping them informed, answering their questions, and guiding them through the process, you provide peace of mind. Clients feel more confident knowing that their taxes are in capable hands, and they have a trusted advisor supporting them.

*Anticipating Client Needs: By staying connected with clients, you gain insights into their evolving needs and can tailor your services accordingly. Understanding their financial goals, life events, and changing circumstances allows you to provide personalized advice and proactive tax planning.

*Resolving Issues Promptly: Regular communication with clients allows you to identify and address any issues or concerns promptly. Proactive problem-solving demonstrates your commitment to client satisfaction, building their trust and confidence in your ability to handle their tax matters effectively.

*Building Your Reputation: Satisfied clients are more likely to provide positive reviews and referrals, contributing to your professional reputation. Word-of-mouth recommendations are powerful in the tax industry, and by delivering exceptional service, you can attract new clients and expand your business.

*Differentiating from Competitors: Excellent client service sets you apart from competitors in the tax industry. By making clients feel comfortable throughout the entire process, providing personalized attention, and staying connected, you create a unique value proposition that distinguishes your practice from others.

In summary, satisfying customers in the tax industry by staying in contact with them, keeping up with their tax updates, and ensuring they feel comfortable throughout the entire process is essential. It strengthens client relationships, builds loyalty, enhances the client experience, provides peace of mind, allows you to anticipate client needs, resolves issues promptly, contributes to your reputation, and helps you differentiate from competitors. By prioritizing client satisfaction, you establish a solid foundation for long-term success in the tax industry.

STEP 8: Process of prep Fees (Importance of discussing cost and the Difference between e-filing and traditional tax refund)

I always let my clients know upfront how much my prep fees are usually ranging between so that there is never any confusion. By letting your clients know upfront the prep fees let's them know you are professional and not trying to get over on them. I always give my clients their quote and then include how much would be taken out for the fees so that I'm fully transparent with them and they aren't lost when their taxes arrive and they see a different amount than told.

1. Pricing Transparency: Clearly defining and communicating your tax preparation fees is essential to establish transparency and avoid misunderstandings with clients. Clients appreciate knowing upfront what services they will receive and how much they will be charged for those services.

2. Fair Compensation: Determining appropriate prep fees ensures that tax professionals are fairly compensated for their expertise and the services provided. It allows you to

account for the time, resources, and knowledge required to accurately prepare tax returns and navigate complex tax regulations.

3. Compliance with Regulations: In the tax industry, there are regulations and guidelines governing the disclosure and charging of tax preparation fees. Understanding and adhering to these regulations helps maintain compliance and ensures ethical and professional practices.

4. Value for Services Rendered: Clients expect to receive value for the fees they pay. By setting fair and competitive prep fees, you can demonstrate the value of your services and expertise, ensuring that clients feel they are receiving quality assistance with their tax matters.

5. E-filing Efficiency: E-filing offers numerous advantages over traditional refund methods. It allows for faster processing, reducing the time it takes for clients to receive their refunds. E-filing also minimizes errors by using automated checks and electronic data transmission, leading to more accurate and efficient tax return submissions.

6. Increased Accuracy: E-filing helps reduce errors in tax returns by minimizing manual data entry and providing built-in validation checks. This decreases the likelihood of mistakes that could lead to delayed refunds or IRS inquiries. As a result, clients can have greater confidence in the accuracy of their tax filings.

7. Faster Refunds: E-filing generally results in faster refunds compared to traditional refund methods, such as mailing paper returns. Clients appreciate the convenience and speed of receiving their refunds electronically, which can contribute to their overall satisfaction with your services.

8. Environmentally Friendly: E-filing is a more environmentally friendly option compared to traditional refund methods that involve printing and mailing paper returns. By promoting e-filing, you can support sustainability efforts and reduce paper waste.

In summary, understanding and effectively managing the process of preparing fees and differentiating between e-filing and traditional refund methods are important in the tax industry. It ensures transparency, fair compensation, compliance with regulations, value for services rendered, efficient tax processing, increased accuracy, faster refunds, and environmental sustainability. By navigating these aspects effectively, you can provide a seamless and satisfactory experience for your clients while maintaining professional standards in the tax industry.

www.ingramcontent.com/pod-product-compliance
Lightning Source LLC
Chambersburg PA
CBHW062300290526
45794CB00006B/2639